FROM THE EDITOR

Story Telling is pleased and proud to present this work by Richard Seal, who since the inception of the series has been a constant subscriber.

We wish to confirm all the text is original and written by Richard himself also none of the work printed here is a duplicate of his prose we have published previously.

Percy Chattey

STORY TELLING ELEVEN

Living Now

By Richard Seal

Published by

Percychatteybooks Publishing

ISBN 978 1 9998869 7 4

Copyright Richard Seal 2018

Richard Seal has inserted his right under the Copyright, Designs and Patents Act, 1988, to be identified as the author of this work.

Hello, my name is Richard Seal I was Born in Sutton Coldfield in December 1967. I started writing poetry and short stories in my teenage years, encouraged by an inspirational teacher, Roger Langley.

Having worked as a Civil Servant, counsellor and then a teacher, my wife Sandra and I moved to Spain in 2014 to embark on a new adventure.

All the poems and stories in this collection have been written since we started enjoying life and feeling revitalised in the Hondon Valley, Alicante.

Recently I have found myself reflecting on the thirty years which have passed since my book 'Shivering in the Sun' was published in July 1988, hence this new work.

Life is all a dream, let's enjoy it before the arrival of the cold light of day.

Richard Seal
1 July 2018

For Sandra – always

"Life is a stick of rock - sweet, hard and shot through with unintelligible words."

School trip sees mind drift to dead arms, girls giggling, teacher's call for calm.

Happiest Days

So many adults seem to say that their school days were the happiest of their lives, but the experience for Diana is unpleasant and painful in so many ways: bullies have a lot of fun at her expense, often laughing at her dress sense, calling her dense, pulling at pigtails, flicking ears. Even so-called friends tease her for being 'weird' and look down their noses. If this is as good as it got for adults, they must have miserable lives!

Weekends are haunted always by the hideous spectre of Sunday night. There seems to be more than one of them in every week: involving a dreaded bath, depressing TV viewing before an early bed. The girl often lies awake contemplating Monday's double maths, the awful gym class and an undeserved telling off by Mrs Smith. She wonders if this particular evening will remain grim, uninspired throughout her life.

While life between the hours of nine and four is frequently full of fears, sometimes a few tears, when Diana gets home true joyfulness appears. Her dad always finds something to laugh about and then ruffles her blond hair, mum listens with love and warmth, and even her brother and sister show in little ways that they care. Feeling safe, valued, and calm of mind requires no spectacles of a rose-coloured kind.

The first day of the holidays always feels special, and ripe with the potential for fun: riding bikes, going on hikes down country lanes or up in the hills with a packed lunch made by mum! It cannot even be spoiled by any encroaching thoughts of the last day: tedious homework not done, revision avoided and studying ignored - the things childhood days have never really been intended for.

Flying above the clouds makes Diana want to shout so loud with unbridled joy at being so high up and far away from the miserable teachers and spiteful girls who kick her satchel, jeer, sneer, and mock her love of fairies, unicorns, mermaids .. The girl may not have travelled abroad yet but she does not see why not actually being in a plane should stop her soaring towards heaven, and reaching the summer sky.

....

Left Field

Wendy always felt out
of the left field: dollies'
limbs all turn-twisted,
make-up grim gothic:
liked magenta dresses,
black and white stripes
on high heeled shoes.
Now daughter delights
and shares mum's taste
in favourite shirts filled
with vivid hues, or bold
silver-gold Alice bands.
Both appreciate passion
for purple polka dots.

Trying On

Struggling under the weight of several bags, Mark shifted his weight from one of his flat feet to the other and endeavoured to lean back against a rack of jackets without causing it to collapse. The gents' toilets were out of order and he was not sure if he could get away with popping into the ladies' without being noticed. He would rather have been almost anywhere else on a hot Saturday afternoon at the end of August than in a busy clothes shop.

He reflected that he had hated shopping since childhood, especially when it involved trying any clothes on. To this day, he still loathes the sensation of trousers pinching flesh, trying to squeeze them over his thighs, and feeling so ashamed and blaming himself for being super-sized. Mark felt a little puzzled, but smiled seeing his daughter's joy as she headed for the changing rooms without any signs of gloom. Rosie did not look depressed at the prospect of sampling skirts or a summer dress.

Moving on to the shoe shop, Mark shudders at memories of the end of the summer holidays and dreaded trips with his mum to buy sensible shoes for school. He felt and still feels such a fool in these places. The grim assistants armed with shoe horns had seemed resolved to raise his embarrassment levels. What made matters worse was that he had suffered blushing seeing a girl from his class just as his mother decided to tell him off ...

Suddenly deciding to take pity on his daughter, Mark grabs the first pair of acceptable-looking shoes in her size which come to hand, hoping that his wife will understand. The man fails to notice that Rosie looks disappointed to be leaving the shop so quickly.

Snuggled

Loves snuggling deep into jumpers,
chunky, woollen, and well wrapped
up in his cosy vest and shirt layers.
Childhood home was freezing cold,
with its frosted-up windows, breath
visible indoors and inadequate heat
barely generated by gas fires' bars.
As an adult feels stifled in the sauna
of a centrally-heated house, hating
tee shirts worn during winter months.
Private glow of glee when the boiler
breaks on Christmas Eve - impossible
for an engineer to come for two days:
Huddles, cuddles .. totally unfazed.

....

Saturday Morning Picture Show

AS A CHILD OF THE NINETEEN SEVENTIES, DAN HAD LOVED
SATURDAY MORNING MOVIE MAGIC AT HIS LOCAL CINEMA:
HAVING A GREAT TIME LARKING AROUND IN THE DARK WITH
HIS SCHOOL FRIENDS, BARELY WATCHING THE SCREEN, IN
THE COMFORTING SUGAR-WARMTH OF POPCORN AND
CANDY FUG. THE CARTOON AND SUPPORTING FEATURE
OFTEN PASSED HIM BY BEFORE EVERYONE SETTLED DOWN
(TO A DEGREE) TO WATCH THE MAIN FEATURE. HE
WONDERED WHY THERE WERE SO MANY ELVIS FILMS AND
ALL THE WESTERNS SEEMED TO BE MUCH THE SAME,
USUALLY STARRING JOHN WAYNE.

RETURNING TO THIS PRECIOUS PLACE MANY TIMES IN HIS
TWENTIES, DAN LOVED TO GET LOST IN THE BIG SCREEN,

ENVELOPED BY SHARED TRANCE, ENHANCED BY LUXURIATING IN SOFT-FOCUS NOSTALGIA. HE WAS OVERJOYED TO FIND THAT MOST OF THE CRAMPED AND TATTY FIXTURES AND FITTINGS REMAINED, ALTHOUGH IT WAS NOT QUITE THE SAME SOMEHOW WITHOUT THE AGED USHERETTE HE REMEMBERED FROM HIS CHILDHOOD - HE HAD BOUGHT SO MANY ICE CREAMS FROM HER TRAY, BEFORE JOINING HIS MATES IN THROWING THE WRAPPERS THROUGH THE PROJECTOR BEAM.

BY HIS THIRTIES, DAN WAS ONLY ABLE TO VISIT THE CINEMA OCCASIONALLY, BUT EVERY TIME WAS A SPECIAL OCCASION. HE NOW PREFERRED A QUIET CORNER AT THE BACK OF THE ROOM WHICH SEEMED TO BE RESERVED JUST FOR HIM. DIET SUSPENDED FOR A COUPLE OF HOURS, HE RELISHED THE PROSPECT OF TACKLING HIS LARGE BAG OF CHOCOLATE PEANUTS AND RAISINS. THE MAN DID NOT MIND WHAT FILM HE WAS WATCHING, HE WAS JUST GLAD TO BE THERE, TO FEEL THAT FAMILIAR SHIVERY THRILL AS HE HUGGED HIMSELF AND RELAXED SITTING BESIDE THE VELVET CURTAIN, HEAD RESTING AGAINST HIS OWN PERSONAL PURPLE PILLAR.

HAVING SPENT MUCH OF HIS YOUTH ENAMOURED OF HIS BELOVED CINEMA, DAN WENT ON TO SPEND HIS FORTIES FIGHTING TO PRESERVE AND PROTECT ITS ART DECO FACADE; IT WAS A LONG, HARD ROAD - MANY MEETINGS AND LETTERS WERE REQUIRED BEFORE THE NECESSARY PERMISSIONS WERE SECURED AND THE BUILDING COULD FINALLY BE SAVED. A VAST' STATE-OF-THE-ART SHOPPING MALL NOW STANDS ON THE SITE ... THE CINEMA BURNED TO THE GROUND ON THE EVE OF THE MAN'S FIFTIETH BIRTHDAY - THE WIRING, OLD AND FAULTY, TOOK THE BLAME.

Concentrate

Old bottle untouched, neglected,
lost at the back of the cupboard
reminded the woman how much
she had loved an orange squash
as a girl, so thirsty having played
with her dolls or friends, hair wild
abandoned to curls; perfect drink
to sip or swig on a summer's day
while dodging persistent wasps ...
Slightly sad at thought its appeal
may have passed, squash passé
these days - regretfully it seems
a bit too late for this concentrate.

,,,,,,,

Pudding with custard

brings back memories of dinner

ladies with steel scoops

School Trip

With a double-seat to herself on the front row of the packed coach, Hannah frowns as she looks around in vain for a window to open. It is an unusually warm day, and there is no curtain to shade her from the sun. The driver has popped out for a rather long quick cigarette break before the start of the school trip. Feeling a trickle of sweat down her back, she loosens the top button of her blouse, and sits back. Her mind drifts to past days out with little boys giving each other dead arms, a gaggle of girls giggling furtively, and the harassed teacher calling for some calm at the back.

Hannah smiles at thoughts of the packed lunch in her bag. She relives childhood smells, tastes of chocolate spread or peanut butter thickly spread on sliced white bread. On excursions there always seemed to be a heady fug of sweaty kids and sandwiches of stinky egg and mayonnaise which seemed to be on the turn, tepid fizzy drinks and sticky sweets. Her mother had prepared lovely food, the girl's favourite was ham, cheese and tomato rolls, with a shiny apple. Everyone in the family, and even visitors, ate better than mum; she settled for leftovers, less than their dogs, cats and even the table she dressed for the birds.

While all her friends marvelled at the monkeys clambering up bars and branches, lions and tigers scowling prowling up and down in cramped spaces, Hannah hated the visits to zoos. She felt depressed, sad, ashamed, and could never bring herself to stand close, get involved, or look into the captive creatures' faces. The worst thing was the sight of birds who seemed so enraged by having to endure hateful lives shut in a cage. Chided by teachers when she tried to turn away, the girl had wanted to cry and put her hands over her face. Even now, she clenches her fists and grinds her teeth at these painful memories.

The half hour journey passes uneventfully, the children are a little on the lively side but there do not seem to have been any major disagreements or fights en route. Having dozed slightly, Hannah now feels her spirits lifting as the bus drives straight past the entrance to that familiar zoo and heads for the adventure park. This primary school teacher had no hesitation in deciding that her class would have more fun on scary rides and water slides, and felt sure that they would be more likely to retain joyful recollections of the experience.

....

Waif

A waif-like young woman
standing, smiling, looking
slight in sunshine, framed
by her tall sisters in a black
and white picture appears
bent brittle, fit only to fade
away, crumble to fine dust
fifty years on. But take pity
on fragile lady at your peril:
the fire storm still rages on
in pale eyes. Consideration
and caution would be wise;
compliance, respectfulness
are enough to do the trick.
Otherwise you can expect
a big whack from her stick.

Loop the Loop

Since he was a boy, Andy has loved to subject himself to the delicious terror of an afternoon spent sampling the scariest attractions at theme parks. He luxuriates in the addictive adrenaline rush, and is more than happy to use his children as an excuse to go as often as possible. The man sometimes wonders whether the kids would rather be at the cinema, playing computer games or hanging out with their friends. He consoles himself by thinking that they could do those things anytime, whereas these thrills are the stuff of memories.

Andy is held in the tight roller coaster car by abject fear, the steel bar crushing his stomach. Tension builds with the clanking crawl up the track to reach the agonising teetering point. Then comes a thunder rush of blur, colour, freeze frames, white noise. Breathing is suspended around the loop-the-loop, with visions of plunging, metal crunching into a twisted heap. The wavering man emerges, pale and sweating from the ride; survival is quietly celebrated by rejoining the queue.

While Karen stands, smiling, with their daughter on the sidelines, Andy takes their excited son along to join him in embracing the heady cocktail served up by dodgem cars: head spin, stomach flip, arms flailing, and the faint-hearted wailing, on the bash, crash whiplash smash. As the chuckling man staggers back towards the ladies, his nausea held just barely at bay, he is delighted that the boy enjoyed himself, and suggests it must be time for some candy floss.

The turning point comes on the Big Wheel. Andy's pulse picks up pace, then begins to race as the ride shudders to a halt while he and his daughter are at the highest point. He can feel the carriage rocking on its axle in the stiff breeze, creaking metal fixings straining while the mechanism's teeth grind below. Suddenly his stomach lurches and the child's hand is squeezed a little too hard. While the little girl is giggling and pointing at the view, the man starts whispering in terror to himself in a battle to stop himself from jumping out.

Safely back down to earth, Andy turns away to be sick, while the children start making enquiries about ice cream vans. For a few minutes, the man wonders if he will be able to face anything more exciting than the swings and roundabouts after this experience. However, any fears that zoos and museums might be his lot from now on are dismissed after a sit down, cup of tea and plate of fish and chips. He spots a new attraction, gets a second wind, and the whole family are keen to join him on 'Oblivion'.

....

Card

**Looked at and then past
roses and flowery verse
on each oversized card ...
Always hard - No words
come close to capturing
sleeping partner's foot
hooked around his leg,
fingers tightening slowly
on his arm when body
shifts slightly. What more
to say for two Valentines
who celebrate every day?**

Headlong

Jenny has always insisted that her young family makes an annual pilgrimage to the Lincolnshire beach that she had loved visiting on her own childhood holidays. The East coast resort seems to get more charmingly broken down every year. She rejoices in the dilapidated wooden beach huts with their flaking paint, and the old-fashioned cafes with weather-beaten signs and their scent of candy floss, hamburgers and fish and chips. The woman still finds so much joy in the down-at-heel amusement arcades with their aged one-armed bandits, creaking penny falls and pinball machines from a bygone age. She even loves seeing the tacky gift shops, some of which are just about clinging on against the tide, while others have already been boarded up.

Every sharp gust of blustery August wind takes her back a couple of decades to happy afternoons spent huddling behind the windbreak, with Dad in his second best suit and Mum clad in a plastic raincoat, each with a hand on a pole to stop their canvas shelter from blowing away. Jenny and her older siblings would sit or crouch on the slightly too small tartan rug, clutching their sandy sandwiches and cans of warm fizzy drink. All adorned in towels and shivering in their swimming costumes, they would train their gazes on the sky, straining to spot a gap in the heavy clouds - so desperate to seize the chance of a quick dip in the sea once the drizzle let up a little.

Sitting on the familiar beach now beside her nonplussed husband, who has finally insisted that they will be going to Spain next year, Jenny keeps a close eye on their children playing nearby. The twins seem to be quite happy looking for shells at the water's edge, each girl with her own pink bucket, trying to find bigger or prettier ones than the other, to bring back to show off to their mum. The boys are building something strange in the sand while simultaneously intent on digging the deepest hole possible. Once their sand creation has collapsed, one of them is sure to end up down in the hole's cold wetness, either laughing or crying.

Turning her freckled face to the sun, Jenny reflects that she would love to lay down her flask of tea, discard the carefully-prepared picnic, cast off her sensible cardigan and strip down to her bikini. She imagines herself hurtling headlong in hysterics towards the sea, trampling on any over-elaborate sandcastles, hurdling bewildered families, kicking sand over bright red sunbathers, and startling a pensioner or two by knocking over their deckchairs. Playing out gay abandon in her mind, the woman behaves wildly in her own inimitable style for a while. As the moment passes with the return of cloud cover, she settles for a little giggle, a private wiggle, snuggle, and a secret smile as she pours orange squash into plastic cups.

....

Hand

Final look at her hand, feeling
confused seeing wedding ring
has been removed ... Grasped,
clasped so often, always strong
and warm to touch, little fingers
tight clutched; Sometimes used
to smack, haul children back,
to check, restrain, encourage
little ones to abstain, remain ...
Flesh now cold, love enfolds.

....

*Girls loved beach with dad
in suit, mum smiling, huddled
snug behind windbreak.*

Still Standing

In the early morning Grandad's bones feel old, so creaky cold and not inclined to do as they are told. Getting out of bed now in slow, painful stages can take Fred ages. Yet his grandson, Wayne, takes longer than him to rise. The teenager looks vaguely surprised to make it downstairs before noon. He knows he will not beat his aged relative to breakfast any time soon.

While Fred groans just slightly when rising in instalments from his favourite chair, he sees Wayne spring from the settee to his feet without hesitation, his ever-present mobile phone clasped in hand. The old man reaches for his stick with a wince at arthritis as the youngster bounds out of the room without thinking to hold the door.

Stepping forward gingerly, Fred takes his son Alan's arm. He feels fit for stumbling, dreads tumbling, and turning an ankle at eighty-one. He pauses, raising an eyebrow at the younger man's moans about a sciatic twinge and persistent grumbling about aching flat feet. Suddenly Grandad feels like he is wearing rather well.

As the three men walk to the local pub together, Fred holds on to his stick and stays close to his son, while Wayne strides a couple of paces ahead of them both. However, at midnight the oldest man is still standing, a little tipsy but relatively steady, and not averse to another pint. He smiles at Wayne, apparently a lightweight, who is leaning on his worse-for-wear father whilst they waver and stagger towards the toilets.

Floating

Watching a lemon slice floating
and chunky cubes of ice chink
bobbing in the glass helps Ian
think about when life seemed
twice as nice. Sitting with her,
gin and tonic seemed sharper,
a piece of cake much sweeter,
even the tablecloth somehow
looked neater. His heavy sigh
acknowledges that Sally was
so much more than his wife -
Her love, humour, beauty, joy
will always invigorate his life.

....

Ladies embrace roles as helpmates: joy for one is happiness doubled

Typewriter

The little girl so loved her typewriter, she often sneaked off with it and hid away in the walk-in cupboard in her parents' room. None of her siblings were allowed in the vicinity of this special friend who captured Amelia's private feelings. She had tried using pen and paper to write her diary, but it was just not the same; the magic machine in its pink case was her confidante.

In her early teens, Amelia took great delight in the way her typewriter's tip tapping seemed in tune with the rhythm of her emotions, the bell ringing out in joyful jubilation at each completed line of verse. She overcame the curse of an 'S' which kept jamming, an 'R' which looked more like a 'P', and never minded tending to its frayed ribbons.

However, the world changed the day that her sister Harriet used the typewriter. The older girl brushed the incident off with barely a shrug, but things were never the same for Amelia again. She often lay awake listening to keys creating messages which were only meant for her, unseen by others. The words stayed in her head, making her feel excited, scared.

Amelia now often stops in the middle of word processing, staring at her computer screen. The cursor seems to blink at her blankly; impassive, not caring about the musings of a middle-aged would-be novelist. The typewriter had been so different. The girl had said nothing to her mum about what the machine told her, and decades on those declarations have still not gone. She knows she can never tell anyone.

Seven

Smiles recalling his wife's deep love

of number seven. Perhaps she felt

its luck might just lead her one day

to the enigmatic gates of Heaven ..

Six of anything was just not enough

with eight or nine a little too much.

Her husband's memories focus now

on seeing arched brow, a wide grin

as she relished the perfect number

of World Wonders and Deadly Sins.

Spice-Rack

They had had a good innings
of course, the adult son told
himself whilst tackling the task
of clearing his parents' house ...
Wonderful memories linger on
in hearts and minds, loved ones
are not really gone he whispered
into a bin liner full of old clothes;
Little did he know that the thing
to make him crack would be
the home-made spice-rack.

....

Message

Jeanette has always loved taking time out to come down to Brighton beach alone. Sitting on the rocks awhile, looking out to sea, feeling invigorated by its spray, she embraces feeling so deliciously small. The surf whips up, hissing its derision; regrouping, it has formed a fist to pummel stone into submission over centuries. She is a piece of driftwood, sodden, rotten, or a football, burst, and spat out on the beach. In the ocean's timeless fury, she is worth nothing.

On this November day, her body buffeted and face cut by chill winds, Jeanette indulges in lingering over distant, soft-focus memories of a sweet little kiss with Pierre behind the sand dunes, tasting ice cream and bubblegum. They had shared their sweets sitting on a bench, hot hands touching tentatively, fingers probing their paper bag. Through the fluttering and flushing, she had felt their names being shot together through the rock.

When Pierre's holiday had ended and he returned with his parents to Brittany, Jeanette had written him a secret message, illustrated and scented, in broken French. She put it into a bottle, which was launched from this beach. Sometimes she fancies that the precious piece of paper survived, the water opted not to seep in and sink her message, and if he has not received it yet, he might do so one day. Perhaps the man will leave his lush vineyard at the age of ninety and look for her across the ocean.

Salt Cellar

The last time he had seen her
in this restaurant she had been
crying profusely, one large tear
dropping onto their salt cellar.
He had tried but failed to help,
give advice, find a few words
to the wise. Pain-stricken look
in her eyes that day confirmed
that she would not be in touch,
intensity of her sadness being
far too much. Now here alone,
condiments remain untouched.

Perspective

They had been here so often,
in all weathers, sitting together
whilst silently apart, so lovingly
lost in art ... Now alone staring
at his canvas, struck by the rain,
making colours run, knows well
for them there had never been
quite enough sun .. Way beyond
vanishing point, all perspective
has long gone on his only one.
....

Tumbledown

Wherever he lived, somehow
the accommodation over time
seemed to fade, degrade take
an untimely dive where once
the building had felt so alive,
and former inhabitants thrived.
Perhaps Barry had been born
down at heel, scruffy headed,
eternally unkempt, bewildered,
out of place - was it his face,
or personality, demeanour?
No matter - with him around
no-one frowned, but life lost
shape and focus, undoubtedly
became so tatty, tumbledown.

Wasp hovers around table eyeing up her man, ready to move in.

....

Happy Couple

Nick feels so weary seeing his eyes looking so bloodshot and bleary after a long stag night in the pub. He often wonders how he could tell his mates that he does not really like drinking beer, talking about women, football, or fast cars. The man often grits his teeth, seething through a smirk, grieving for precious time not spent with like-minded types over a coffee, discussing books, watching films, and taking turns to be the friend who cooks.

Planned for weeks by her friends, the Hen Night's arrival filled Cathy with a deep- seated sinking dismay. A few quiet drinks had descended quickly into hitting vodka hard, tequila slammers, and falling in and out of nightclubs. Adjusting her fixed grin, she had suffered in silence amid all the whoops and hilarity, whilst adorned by a red L-Plate. She would have much preferred to curl up on the sofa, listen to some classical music and sip tea over feline chat.

How much had the happy couple drunk last night? The bar staff were not keeping count or judging customers on the amount they consumed, as long as they kept it down and avoided starting a fight. Nobody had noticed a girl sitting quietly crying, or cared about the man being sick in the car park. They kept the tills ringing. Those in service kept calm, professional, offering everyone a winning smile and all the ladies ice and a slice.

The groom stands still, staring straight ahead, trying not to shake in dark suited sobriety. His mouth is getting dryer while his pale face is soaked, and white shirt darkening with sweat. The bride's big day started with a cold compress, some weak tea, and soluble pain solutions. The couple swallow hard, so green queasy in front of rows of smiling faces. Feeling tender, second hand and breaking wind in front of the vicar was not what had been planned.

....

One-Up

Whatever Helen had to say
her colleague Jane turned things her way:
Without fail, she had done it first;
if yours was bad, then hers was worse.

To Helen's flat, Jane had a house;
A boyfriend topped by loving spouse;
A break in England met with scorn
as Jane preferred to be airborne.

When common cold was trumped by flu
there seemed no more that she could do;
Then Helen's cancer was swept aside
when Jane collapsed at work and died.

Helpmates

Jean and Janet have spent all their lives taking every chance to help each other: At school, their homework was shared, knowledge and ideas pooled; calm words were always spoken if one of them was scared; boyfriend advice was freely dispensed, often with a hug; decisions were discussed; and any favour never needed to be asked for twice. As they went on to become wives and mothers, each woman became a special aunt to the children of the other. While the passing years have inevitably taken their toll, the elderly ladies embrace their roles as mutual helpmates. Nothing is too much trouble: joy for one is happiness doubled.

For these two soul mates, walking together and talking to each other was always such fun; Strolling through the decades at a leisurely pace, never dreaming of running; so happy sunning themselves while shooting the breeze, taking their ease, preferring to chew the fat about their beloved families and dear dogs and cats. Finally, their legs have given out, but neither of them really care about that because it has given them a new interest to share. Jean loves to show off her range of ornate steel-capped canes, while Janet cannot wait to demonstrate her new 'bells and whistles' wheelchair, top of the range.

Richard Seal in Story Telling

Every Wednesday the ladies continue to sit happily sipping milky coffee in their favourite corner cafe, which has survived somehow albeit greatly changed since their youth. They say little to each other; both smile slightly as a middle-aged waitress bustles past their table, walking comically fast, and the busy sounds of different generations' background chitter chatter natter drift past. Just one look with a hint of a wink and a familiar furtive grin, a cheeky playfulness within, is all it takes to reflect the fun, warmth, happiness and love - comforting and undemanding - between the best of friends of more than sixty years standing.

....

Umbrella

He left a small black one
on the last train as it began
to rain - a familiar refrain:
His girlfriend had lost one
with pink flowers, on the bus
during heavy April showers ...
He got wetter before finding
another, much bigger, better
for a couple to shelter under.

*Took wrong turn in life
awhile: blind alleys, stop signs.
Now found open road.*

Buried

Mike can feel himself slipping further and further down under the weight of a collapsing marriage, the spectre of impending redundancy, huge mortgage payments, the loan for his new car, and the kids' exorbitant school fees. Living well beyond his means has sunk him into a pit, he is slowly being buried alive. Each night, lying awake in bed for hours, the man feels burned out, wanting to shout, surrounded by dark clay ...

In sleep, he becomes weightless, timeless, drifting through space; now displaced without form or sense of alarm, moving beyond calm into a realm lacking thought. Then dim figures from the past mutate, degenerate into shade-faded creatures of hate, bringing naked fright in the very deepest dead of night. A flesh tremor sent down his spine feels so intense whilst he is lying prone, without any form of defence.

Concealed behind the curtains or under the bed, lingers a sickening dread, a fear of death, nothingness and beyond. A slight figure appears nightly as a streak - A grime-grey shroud of cloud dissipating into a dirty stain. Mike asks himself in fleeting moments of consciousness if this shadow lady huddled in the corner, pulling at her long grey hair, imploring, trying to scream, rising to fall, is actually there at all.

As a small black cat sidles underneath his bed, the darkness gathers around cobwebs to form a tiny figure in a shapeless hat; she hovers above the stricken man awhile; she could be kindly with a half smile, but falters a moment in black, green to grisly mean. Puss emerges in the fading night - his enigmatic magic is, for now, dissipated by scant daylight.

Heavy rain and a loud branch crack end the nightmares, but not the interminable feeling of blackness. The morning returns him to the daytime show awhile - A range of roles to be performed with diligence, vigour; each of his faces are different, shifting, and always presented with a valiant smile. Mike knows only too well that the next night will attack, change tack, bringing many different realities back

... Submerged, going under, soil sputtering in his mouth, heavy cold-sweating, limbs like lead, he is yearning now for the last spadeful to be thrown over his head.

....

Find glimpses of time undefined, a drifting peace in silence, dreamless.

Taxi Driver

Emma felt exhausted as she hauled her heavy bag off the train. The platform was windswept and nearly deserted that chilly September evening, and she was looking forward to the prospect of a long bath and a large glass of chilled white wine. The young woman was glad that she had phoned ahead for a taxi to take her back to her flat.

The driver looked at Emma with hooded eyes as he lifted her bag into the back of his car. As she took the seat beside him she noticed that the interior smelled vaguely of coconut. She half expected to see a couple of furry dice hanging from the mirror. As usual the passenger was not quite sure how much to say to her companion, and whether she should open a conversation about something safe like the weather. He saved her the trouble by speaking first.

"Did you find any inspiration on your trip, miss?"

"I'm sorry?" He continued "You have the air of a writer about you, if you don't mind my saying so."

"Well, yes, actually I am a writer, sort of .. "

"We all are in our own way ." He was silent for a few moments before continuing "There are so many stories to be told, don't you think?"

"Yes. I have written quite a few poems and a few short stories over the years, but would like to try my hand at writing a novel."

"Poetry is pure. It contains moments of eternity held suspended in images." Emma shot him a glance, but he remained focused on the road. "I know what you mean, but people don't really seem to value poetry these days ."

"I wonder which people you mean, and what their concept of value looks like?"

Emma was a little flummoxed. "Well, poetry collections don't sell, or even get published."

"Oh I see. These people might be more interested in buying first novels by new writers. Did you find what you were looking for whilst walking across the windswept moors?"

"Do my clothes give me away that much? I know I'm not looking too glamorous at the moment. Yes, I went away to be at one with nature and stayed at a remote bed and breakfast last night. I came away with very little for my book, but it was a good breakfast!"

"Where do you usually write, and when do you find yourself visited by the elusive Muse?"

"Actually, at surprising times really. I often get ideas at night and need to switch on the light to jot them down. Or things come to me when I'm waiting for a train or a plane, sitting in a cafe alone. "

"Or perhaps during a conversation with a stranger?"

"Yes .. I only need a line or two, or even just a few words to get started sometimes"

"Creativity comes in the silence, magic resides in the space between feeling and thought."

"I guess so, I hadn't thought about it like that before. God knows how the writing process works!"

"Does He?" Emma paused. "I don't know. What do you think?"

"Human beings need to frame their existence, give it some structure and narrative to help their lives make some kind of sense. We tell stories that heal, colourful tales like those to be found in The Bible for example."

"Yes, I'm uneasy about Heaven, Hell and the afterlife but I wouldn't call myself an atheist."

"Why call yourself anything, is a label necessary? All we need to know is that there is a great unknown, so much beyond the realm of human comprehension, and that's enough."

"That's true. What comes afterwards can't be any worse than what came before we arrived, I suppose. ... If we are really here at all, that is."

The car stopped, and the man turned to her with a smile. "Well, we're here now, miss. My next fare is just round the corner, just off the high street."

Emma felt dazed and strangely bereft for a moment as she stood on the pavement and watched the man drive away into the darkness. A charge started to run through her body. The bath and the wine were no longer required. She went inside and got straight down to work.

....

Deer moving through woods stops dead, hearing snap of trap on hunter's ankle.

Fell

**Whilst he fell for her first time
they had met, the problem was
he kept on falling: into despair,
a void that he could not avoid.
Her assertion that he should
snap out of it left him reeling,
concealing the profound pain
while her urging to get a grip
caused his will to live to slip ..
Despite both still being there,
neither now seemed to care.**

....

Weight

Having struggled with her weight since childhood, by the time she reached her thirties Ellen had become obsessively determined to conquer the flab. She decided to transform herself into an avid swimmer. She did not care how many hours she needed to spend in the pool, pushing herself to total exhaustion, counting each length, battling her failing strength by trying extra hard to improve, and remove any excess fat. Her weight-loss plan had been going so well, until it was sent off track for a while by a mild heart attack.

Ellen feels embarrassed wearing her bikini on the beach, and as she sits on a towel and applies sun tan lotion she cannot help the onset of scarlet cheeks sizzling fearing any scrutiny of her figure. She imagines fat rolls bulging through her tight costume, and fears the spectre of unsightly stretch marks. A thick-set man standing nearby, sporting a beer belly, appears as if he could be weighing her up, giving her a visual body frisk, although she cannot be sure whether he is actually looking at her, or through her searching for someone else in the crowd.

The man in question, Alan, had been trying in vain to spot an unoccupied patch of sand. He was wearing a trademark loose-fitting tee shirt, preferring not to expose his torso. Steadily piling on the pounds since his youth, puppy-fat had become plumpness, then obesity. Reaching the stage of indulging by stealth and avoiding seeing the doctor, he was prevailed upon to take action. The man eventually got used to fruit and vegetables, and begrudgingly gave up eating most sweet things. Nowadays, staring deep into a bottle of water, or contemplating a green salad, he reflects on decades of excess. Despite his diet-related health problems, there are no regrets. Would he do it all over again given the chance? You bet!

Sitting two towels down from Ellen, Jemma scowls and bridles as she replays years of skinny jibes, jests about flat chests, barbs about her garb. Her friends may well cherish their cuddliness and curves, but how dare they have the nerve to poke fun or be mean to someone who is healthily slim, slender, lean. Her stomach is taut, waistline kept under control: Lunchtimes involve lettuce, celery sticks, humus, and even a little dark chocolate with its enriching antioxidants. Jemma allows herself a secret smile, suddenly feeling quietly smug. She is snug in a size four, without any slow metabolism moans; she is so proud of her bones.

....

Car under bent tree, couple in mangled wreckage still with limbs entwined.

One Foot

Knows well if he can keep
walking alone, head down,
without a phone, steering
clear of people's whinging,
and their withering moans,
he will stand half a chance
of escaping awhile chaotic
mind, briefly leave behind
fevered fretfulness, bother.
His focus, as ever, remains
exclusively on putting one
foot in front of the other.

....

*A favourite pastime
is loving being here now
not over there, elsewhere*

Painting

The painting had been hanging on the wall in the living room for as long as Adam could remember. After his parents died, he had toyed with the idea of taking it down, but the picture had by now become too much a part of the fabric of the house and his life to be removed. He found himself increasingly entranced by the sensations of joy and foreboding that it engendered.

As a child, stuck indoors alone on rainy days, he would enjoy taking a leisurely stroll down the painting's long, winding country lane, stopping at the gate and climbing the stile to get a closer look at the sheep in the field, and gaze up at the tufty clouds. At other times he would take a break from his homework to lie atop one of the haystacks on a hazy July afternoon, a piece of straw in his mouth, contentedly lost in daydreams.

However, the onset of teenage years began to take him into some of the shady areas at the frame's edges. A gathering storm was long threatened by thickening clouds. Eventually a strange scarecrow appeared in the middle of the field, and the unsettling contortions of his mouth and limbs led to some of the sheep departing, while those that remained started to look on edge, and huddled closer together.

In adulthood, the heavens often opened and he would become engulfed by the deluge. Although the rain abated from time to time, and the breeze brought temporary refreshment, the sun never really appeared again. The shepherd gradually lost his smile, before vanishing from the scene altogether. While Adam could not fully escape the scarecrow's scrutiny, he took refuge under a solitary tree, which was finally struck by lightening just after his fiftieth birthday.

Portal

Each night feels fascinated
entering a portal between
being awake and asleep,
lingering awhile on fringes
before dropping too deep.
Half conscious, tries to stay
upright instead of tripping
off a curb, stalling a feeling
of falling to keep one foot
both sides of dividing line.
Captures glimpses of time
undefined, a drifting peace
within silence, dreamless.

Life Story

Memory nearly full, time
felt right to capture
and release life in
writing. Childhood fell
away, as fingers brushed
keys, to the outbreak
of war. Screen flickered
as youth channelled
through marriage, children
to middle age. Over Caps
Lock, around Bold font
time skirted. Thoughts
and feelings smothered
memories, bleeding into
dreams. He pressed 'Escape'.

Arrival

Teresa always loves the process of taking her case down from the top of the wardrobe, and lingering with relish over the packing. She gets so excited about embarking on yet another journey to a far-flung foreign place: An ancient city full of mystery perhaps; or a visit to the tiniest of beaches, so secluded; remote mountain trails with weird animals included; or a village where no tourists have intruded, which has somehow managed to evade the capture of any maps.

Always opting for a 'meal deal' at the airport, Teresa never feels enthusiastic about the selection, doubting whether the sandwiches would stand up to a close inspection. She is uninspired by the choice of crisps or cake, but feels happier with bottled water, a nod in the direction of healthy eating. Other food options, however, are not considered - there is no time, she has no desire to be late; besides there is a queue at her gate.

The young woman had not been able to believe her luck at finding such a cheap flight online. Teresa did not mind paying the additional cost to take a bag, and then a little more to select a seat (an emergency exit was extra of course). She treats herself to a couple of costly gin and tonics as she wryly reflects that it could have been worse: The airline did not take the chance to exact a charge for oxygen consumption in advance.

Reclining her seat, Teresa is determined to embrace the long-haul flight. For eight hours she disappears into dreams and fantasies, running her own action -packed inner movie scenarios through the night. However, adrenaline rushes and anticipation builds rapidly as the plane touches down; She hopes to head out and quickly get lost in the realm of her imagination. This traveller always thrives, survives and yet she never really leaves or arrives.

....

Potato

Potato aspires to rise
above his fellow spuds:
He will not lose his grip
to slip into being chipped;
He refuses to be foiled
by being boiled, or raise
a toast to being roasted;
sautéed is not okay, fried
to be derided, no esteem
gained in being creamed ..
Instead, seeks special thrill
as key part of vodka team
in three day brew and distil.

Bun prepared: brown hair hoisted tight, taut, trapped aloft. Only wisps escape.

Last Orders

Feeling weary at the prospect of another long week, landlord Mick sighed heavily as he slipped the bolts and opened the double doors of the small country pub at just after noon. Two of the elderly regulars, arriving dead on time as always, had already knocked on the doors a couple of times and shuffled glumly past him, mumbling under their breath about the landlord being five minutes late again. They watched him in sullen silence as he pulled the first of their customary three pints of mild, then they retired to sit in their usual corner, barely speaking to each other.

The Monday lunchtime session was not a particularly busy one, the pub's two rooms were occupied by the usual sprinkling of long-term regulars. There was one stranger present, however, and Mick was surprised to see him appearing to make a beeline for one particular seat. Despite being scrutinised disapprovingly by several of the old timers, the stranger with the inscrutable smile nursed his half a pint of bitter for a considerable period while sitting beneath the prominent 'Charlie's Corner' plaque on the wall.

As three o'clock approached and the lunchtime drinkers drifted away, the landlord was aware that the stranger was the last person remaining. As the man approached the bar, Mick was filled with a disconcerting inner chill. The figure was tall, gaunt and cadaverous, he was wearing a black coat with a hood which cast a shadow over a face which appeared to be somehow both grey and pale. The man fixed him with a blank yet penetrating stare before speaking in a low, guttural voice.

"I have come for Charlie .. " He paused, before adding. "When you see him this evening, I would be much obliged if you would tell him that I will be back to take him at last orders"

Mick could feel his stomach falling as the man spoke. Suddenly he found that he was sweating profusely, the man's heart had started racing and he could not hear anything other than the voice which seemed to permeate his being with inscrutable terror. He spoke tremulously:

"What do you mean?" He paused, uncertainty "Who are you, and where are you planning to take Charlie?"

"My name is Reaper. I have no doubt whatsoever that Charlie will remember me. I met him here in this room fifty years ago, and I told him the date and time when I would return."

"Fifty years ago! What on earth are you talking about? And what makes you think he will agree to go anywhere with you?" Mick was trying to sound confident and composed, but was feeling overwhelmed by a dark sense of foreboding.

The man looked puzzled for a moment, before replying slowly. "There is no choice in this matter, Landlord - it is his time. He will leave here with me tonight"

Before Mick had the chance to say anything else, the man had slipped away into the shadows, disappearing into the heavy gloom of the November afternoon. Locking the doors behind him, the Landlord looked out into the windswept car park. He braced himself against the drizzle-laden breeze, but there was no sign of the man.

Mick felt unsettled and disorientated by his encounter with the stranger. These feelings remained with him over the next couple of hours as he finished clearing up then sat down to have lunch. He debated about whether he should speak to Charlie about the mysterious message when he came in as usual that evening, and if so what would the man think? The Landlord began to think that he could have actually imagined the whole encounter - it had been a busy few weeks after all, he had been feeling under strain and off colour a lot lately. A fortnight's holiday was well overdue, but the brewery kept putting him off as they were struggling to find a relief to cover him.

Still feeling preoccupied when getting ready to open up again at five o'clock, Mick decided to check on the cellar first, as he had had several new barrels delivered that morning and they needed attention. No sooner had he walked down the steps than the door slammed shut. Puzzled and shocked, the Landlord rushed back up to the heavy door to find that it was stuck fast. How could it have blown shut? There were no windows open, and he was the only person on the premises ... Putting his shoulder to the door, Mick tried to force it open time and time again, but it almost felt like someone was pushing with all their strength in the other direction to keep him imprisoned. He could feel the sweat running down his back and sticking to his shirt and his heartbeat and sense of panic rising rapidly.

Finally the door gave way to his pressure and he fell heavily onto the concrete floor at the top of the stairs. There was no one there, but the landlord felt terrified, dazed and very close to losing consciousness. He lay there without moving for a couple of minutes, barely aware of his throbbing knee and grazed elbow, until his breathing had returned to something close to its normal rate.

When he got to his feet again and stumbled back into the bar, Mick could see that things were not right. The fittings, the decoration, the furniture and lighting ... everything around him looked different. The music on the jukebox was unmistakably from the nineteen fifties, and the customers looked different, yet somehow familiar. To a refrain of Elvis Presley singing 'Jailhouse Rock', He squinted, then rubbed his eyes in disbelief - it looked like many of the people were younger versions of the old men he saw in the bar every day. He could feel his insides starting to shrivel up within his body, and wondered if he might be sick.

A young Jim Reynolds approached him and asked for a pint of bitter and one of his cheese and onion cobs "I hope it's fresher than the one I had yesterday," he grumbled.

Mick looked at him for a few moments without replying. "Jim? Is it you."

The young man looked at him defensively, running his hand through thick blond hair which the Landlord assumed must have fallen out a long time ago. "Well, I'm Jim to some of my friends. You can call me James." Placing a few old pennies on the counter, he gave Mick a mirthless smile, took his sandwich and drink and returned to his seat. He looked back towards the bar a couple of times with an expression of bewilderment.

Mick looked down at the old money, then over at the ancient cash register. There were a few unappetising-looking ham and cheese cobs left in the transparent plastic box on the counter, just like his grandfather had described to him, with a nostalgic grin, many years ago. Nearby there was also a large jar of what he assumed to be pickled eggs, and a smaller one of onions. There was no sign of the credit card machine, no-one was glued to their mobile phone and virtually everyone in both rooms appeared to be smoking.

The Landlord stopped in his tracks when he saw the unmistakable figure of a very much younger and almost fresh-faced looking Charlie Miller sitting in his corner, playing dominoes with friends. He was not wearing his ever-present flat cap, and he was smoking a cigarette instead of his trademark pipe, but he was drinking his usual pint of bitter with a whisky chaser and his heavy-set features and truculent expression were unmistakable.

Suddenly the bar doors opened and the distinctive figure of Reaper, looking exactly the same as when Mick had seen him that lunchtime, walked in purposefully and headed straight for Charlie. Instinctively, he dashed out from behind the bar and seized him before he had a chance to reach his target or say anything to him. The Landlord told the bemused - looking customer to stay back and bundled Reaper out of the pub, but in the process there was a scuffle and Mick received a heavy blow to the face. Before he blacked out, he heard the eerie voice say "I will be back to collect ..."

Finding himself lying on the floor beside the bar door, the Landlord opened his eyes slowly, and focused on the several gnarled faces looking down at him. The men were too feeble to haul the sturdy man back to his feet, but for a few moments they seemed to be almost as concerned about him as they were about the delay in having their evening drinks served up.

"What have you been up to, Mick? Drinking your own profits?"

"Lying down on the job again, you just can't get the staff these days!"

"It's a bit cold for sunbathing, Gaffer! Can't you wait for your annual trip to the Bahamas?"

Mick's heart skipped a beat when he saw old Jim. He grabbed him by the arm "Seriously, Jim, what happened?"

The man looked at him gravely. "You opened the doors then just seemed to collapse on the spot, pass out. How are you feeling now?"

"I'm OK, I think, I just feel a bit confused .. " His head was thumping.

"Are you quite sure? You don't need us to call a doctor?"

"No, thanks." He rubbed his face slowly, then shook his head a couple of times in a vain attempt to clear his thoughts.

"In that case ... " a different voice chimed in " .. Let's get the show on the road. I'm gasping for a pint!"

Smiling now, he walked back into the present-day version of the pub with the men and started pouring their beers. After a busy evening during which he had indulged in a few drinks himself, had a few laughs and got involved in a lot of banter and teasing, Mick was just starting to feel normal again. He was a little puzzled that many of the regulars had not been in that night, and something still felt a bit different about the pub somehow, but he could not put his finger on what it was.

He was about to ring the final bell at eleven o'clock when he looked up to see the shadowy Reaper standing in front of him. His thin lips were twisted into a grim smile.

"Good evening."

Mick felt the colour draining from his cheeks. "I haven't seen Charlie, he hasn't been in tonight"

The stranger shook his head slowly. "No, of course he hasn't. The man died of throat cancer ten years ago." He paused, frowning. "He hasn't been in here for a long time. Perhaps you haven't noticed that he doesn't have a plaque."

Mick could see that there was still a plaque in Charlie's corner, but it looked different and he could not read it from this distance. "What are you saying .. ?"

The stranger fixed the cold gaze on the landlord again. "Jim Reynolds received that accolade a few years ago. He doesn't look particularly grateful to have a corner named after him though, does he?" He cleared his throat before speaking again. "I hope I didn't hurt you with that punch, that's quite a black eye you've got there!"

Mick felt his face gingerly. "I'm fine, no thanks to you! So why have you come in here again then?" He tried to mask his fear with heavy sarcasm. "Aren't you tempted to take your brand of wit and wisdom down the road to the Anchor? They have a Happy Hour on Mondays"

"Why am I here?" The stranger's expression had turned malevolent, and his eyes were black. "It should have been Charlie Miller's time to go now, but you are responsible for changing that, aren't you? All this is down to you. I told you I would be back to collect."

"Collect? Collect what?" Reaper placed a bony hand firmly on Mick's shoulder. "It's last orders, Landlord ... "

Cracks

As a child greatly perturbed
by facing pavement cracks,
not clear which tack to take
when seeing a street lamp
switched on by day, unsure
how to keep anxiety at bay
over ticking clocks, shocks
at constantly dripping taps.
Growing up, began to relax
and embrace OCD, smiling,
tapping every other tree.

....

Check In

Rachel purses her lips as she scans the familiar hotel lobby. She could do with a cigarette, and wonders how long she will be able to give up smoking this time. It is proving difficult for both staff and guests to warm up to the automated check-in machines, and she hates her new 'executive customer assistant' role which involves lurking in the vicinity to help people where needed. Rachel feels that her interpersonal. skills are not being put to best use pressing buttons and scrutinising computer screens. She misses her ex-receptionist friends who have been dispensed with under the company's 'last-in-first-out' redundancy policy, and is just relieved that her old friend Sinead is still there to help keep her sane.

Karen had problems working out how to check in when she arrived, and the assistant had seemed bored and testy when helping her to complete the process, but in all other respects she is enjoying the experience of slipping away for a weekend break in a posh hotel. Entering her room, the woman had thrilled at the sight of little chocolates on her pillow, and embraced the abandonment of a strict diet for some high-fat and sugary room service treats and a bottle of wine for one. She now feels aglow at the prospect of a Saturday to be spent having a pampering manicure, pedicure, massage, and topping it all off with a full body wax.

Frank had felt bemused by the hotel's problematic modern check-in system and the harassed-looking female assistant with the deeply furrowed brow. In many respects the other features of the hotel boast a distinctly retro feel and he indulges himself by enjoying taking a trip back to the nineteen seventies with the beige fringed lamp shades, Apollo wallpaper, and candlewick bedspreads. He had half-expected last night's dinner menu to include prawn cocktail, duck a l'orange, and perhaps even some Black Forest gateau ... Whilst heartened to see that his waiter was moustachioed, his morale dropped just a little when he had not seen any mutton chops.

Dean had barely registered checking in on arrival. Upon waking, the man finds himself helplessly shaking, mistaking another morning for the continuation of dread of an endless night. Fear-frozen in sheets wet with sweat, disappointed that life's ordeal is continuing, his tunnel is interminably dark, with no light at the end. The distant laughter echoing down the stairwell takes him back into the childhood terror of a little girl ghost nightmare: a crying child with blond hair turned white and a darkness behind her dead, blank stare. Even two teenagers running past the door, in hysterics, does not break the spell but rather sinks this anxious wretch deeper into hell.

Sinead sighs as she trudges along the corridors, having been a world-weary chambermaid for nearly two decades. She has hung on in there as the hotel changed from a friendly, family-owned place to a corporate chain, and pushed countless trollies over miles of thin carpets as the years have ticked by. The woman finds few shocks with handcuffs, leather, men in frocks but stains on the sheets seem to be getting worse with foul towels and a toilet curse ... This morning she pauses, a plastic cup in hand - The sight of a dead woman in the bath was not planned. Perhaps it is high time she retired, her soap and shower-caps are no longer required.

Quivering, join swell
of people descending, sucked
down into the Tube.

Man by his car, preens
and checks his lavish plumage.
Blackbird drops a bomb.

Confections

Used to love liberal sprinklings

of salt on every savoury food,

vinegar poured onto his chips;

cream or custard on puddings,

heaped spoons of white sugar

in tea was par for the course.

Eventually his blood pressure

crept up, angina encouraged

him to sample pulses, seeds,

soup that tasted like weeds.

Tried so hard that in the end

happy with vegetables, fruit

and nuts. He now embraced

the rejection of confections.

One June afternoon
light seemed extra bright, coming
from somewhere vivid.

Shot

Sitting in her corner booth, life seems much improved: Elena stares down transfixed, bewitched by the alluring sight of her first expresso of the day. She can barely wait, delighted to anticipate the instant hit of joie de vivre, her taut nerves soothed, outlook on life much improved. Licking her lips before taking a sip, her nervous system flips then trips as she reflects there surely can be no harm in coffee's shot in the arm.

Moving outside to light up over her second cup, Elena lingers over the rich steam, high on the twin hit of the caffeine and nicotine. Her gaze drifts over to a group of young people sitting together at the next table, busy sending text messages to friends elsewhere via phone - happy accessing their social media platforms alone. She frowns to herself, feeling both frustrated and a little sad to hear nothing being spoken.

For a few moments Elena feels rather smug with the thought that she could survive without relying on the Internet, and would be more than happy with her book, a pen and paper should inspiration take her, and paints and canvas at home. Then, as she feels her mobile vibrate, she suddenly wonders what she would actually say if told that her phone was being taken away, or could not be used for a whole day. How would she handle a lack of coffee and fags? The cigarette end is now dropped limply into cold, bitter dregs.

Time Out

From her balcony she could see
that she had captured sunshine
in her courtyard. It was shifting,
drifting a little to accommodate
a fat ginger cat. Long shadows
stretched out across flagstones,
but these were on the periphery,
unable to infiltrate white sunlight.
So intense, rays were allowed
to take time out behind a cloud.

The heather rouses
itself to ripple, while clouds
shift, break and spill sun.

....

Foal in the field shifts
and shivers under blanket.
Baby steps to poise.

Eternal Cat

Watching her tabby cat reclining on his favourite window sill, Sally fantasises that he might have been around since prehistoric times, sidling around dinosaurs and dodging the cavemen. He must have seen so much with the energies and experiences of millennia recycled and then reborn in his timeless eyes. Surely her little James must be eternally wise ...

When he finally passes away, Sally wonders if her precious puss might be laid to rest in the special corner of the iconic British Museum which houses cat mummies - enigmas of centuries, wrapped in bandages upon which faces were drawn. These forms hold the riddles of hieroglyphs, deep-dark secrets of Pharaohs residing in dust with a hint of a purr and the faintest of echoes. Perhaps James was King Tutankhamon's trusted friend, often sitting at the feet of the Boy King, cleaning his paws.

Her cat survived the Great Plague of course, while the Fire of London did not singe his fur; Amber eyes wide, he lounged in the corner of the room watching a tiny spider move while Queen Victoria died. During the World Wars, James passed his time comforting the bereaved. He sidled up to troubled ones, taking his place on a lap, ready to listen without judgement before taking a nap. If a pained person's sleep was disturbed, the cat would come unperturbed; He proceeded through silent kneads, calm resolution reached with feline absolution.

... When James suddenly trains his gaze on her then averts his eyes, Sally knows her own existence is not worth lingering upon. With barely a sniff, Eternal Cat has gone.

....

Walking in mountains,
rocks dent shoe soles, while loose earth
shifts to slip sliding

....

Hamster turns and turns
on wheel, going nowhere fast,
but hay looks comfy.

Scratched

Left a widower when young, losing
a decade to crippling grief, barely
able to handle desperate despair,
Jim is overjoyed finding love again
at fifty. Helen is so loving and kind,
but one thing is on the man's mind:
The lady's cat Pinky, very precious,
loathes him. In the lady's presence
kitty obliges with drilling and purrs,
but when she walks out evil occurs:
The man gets narrow eyes, growling,
bristling fur - He is left in no doubt
that adversary plans to get him out.
Jim will endeavour to win puss over,
but he fears he has met his match;
Pinky wants this particular fixture,
and human's face, to be scratched.

Too Good

Bill and Jean love describing to friends back in Wolverhampton how their Spanish villa is tucked away on a mountain road behind an abandoned ruin, beside a forgotten expanse of wasteland which hosts an occasional sheep or goat, with black trees struggling to yield any olives. They excitedly explain that it is too far for the postman to trek, so they have a village mail box - a space stuffed full of old leaflets, and fiesta flyers from yesteryear, parties probably celebrated with customary joy when the aged local shepherd was just a boy.

Flanked by stunning views, lush almond groves, and fields full of oranges and lemons, Bill and Jean often sit together gazing at the landscape and feel that all this is a bit too good to be true ... However, they know, through the blood red brilliance of the Costa Blanca sunsets, the occasional dog bark carried on the breeze, and the birds which nightly hold the high notes on their twisted boughs, that this is how life is supposed to be.

Sitting in church every Sunday, listening to the service, Bill and Jean are vaguely lost amid Our Lady and saints unknown. They marvel at the Spanish words barely understood but sensed and sampled. A smiling señor and señora on the row in front suddenly turn to clasp their hands, making the couple feel so welcome. Afterwards they enjoy a leisurely lunch with a few Spanish locals, savouring the great value menu del dia with a bottle of vino tinto - Neither dissent at the prospect of time so well spent.

On a late August evening, Bill and Jean stand in the village surrounded by Spanish folk in family clusters, sitting together on rickety chairs hauled out of shuttered houses. The fiesta parade of floats leaves the pair in slack-jawed awe: Flower pot children amble ahead of twenties' flappers, blazing a trail for Hawaiian gyrators; comic characters herald zombies and an underworld cast before the spectacular midnight firework blast. English village fetes seem such distant memories, the couple's life now is a Fandango; They smile at each other and wonder each day who could have spiked their Earl Grey.

Squirrel curses line
loaded with washing. Deft flick
sends shirts puddle-bound.

In abandoned house,
earthy mustiness is framed
by three-legged chair.

Struck

Always loved searing thrill
of the thunder crack, seeing
each forked lightning attack,
relishing shiver tingles shot
up his back. Often wondered
how it would feel on the end
of an electric strike; tempted
to cling to a church steeple
perhaps, or at least shelter
under a tree to be set free.

....

Rocking Horse

Rocking Horse stands still
in Granny's tiny back room.
Saddle, cherry-varnished,
held Mum and twin sisters
in their shriek giggling joy;
Witnessed hair pulls, tears
(and drinks) often spilled.
Silently defying decades,
it guards the house, long
after little girls have gone.

Tortoise

From the living room window, Ann smiled watching the squirrel enjoying the fine afternoon. rolling his nuts, dark eyes sharp and darting, deep in thought about secret burial sites; nearby, the family cat, frozen with a saint's patience, shifted her body, then flattened it as she edged silently towards the intruder. Squirrel dropped his lunch, tail whopping around his shoulders; Cat weighed up her chances then gave a flick and little sniff, before turning tail.

Two hours later a hedgehog skulking around the back garden in dying light of a long spring evening, blinked up at the children standing around, making oohing, cooing sounds. He paused as an elderly lady approached, holding a plate. Having already confused a couple of foxes, sidestepped a big dog and dodged several wasps that day, hedgehog is happy to scoff a tin of the cat's food before scuttling off into the lengthening shadows.

Collecting the empty plate in the almost total darkness, Ann stands for a moment in quiet reflection. Throughout her youth, she had envied her pet tortoise Peter as he settled down in his cosy box to hibernate every year, snuggling in so safe and warm. For him there was no sense of fear, alarm, spending his quiet life calm without braving cold, or having to endure school - The little girl had known that Peter was no fool. And now, while the lady is elderly, weary, slowly fading away, her tortoise is alive to this day. She now has no doubt that little Peter will see her out.

′′′′′′′′

Mossy stones, roses
ancient, the ivy stretching.
Dark privet timeless.

Persian

(i). Dancer (1915-1935)

Dancing was the young woman's all-consuming passion in life. Since she had been a little girl, Kate had lived to seize any opportunity to put on a party dress and dance to any kind of music, even if it was only to the jaunty tunes in her head. She played her parents' radio and all the records in their limited collection endlessly, urging them to buy more. She would jump for joy whenever there was a Friday afternoon country dancing session at her primary school. Without hesitation, she would drag the nearest shy and blushing boy into her arms without a trace of self consciousness.

Kate was a very popular girl, regularly attending friends' parties, but she was far less interested in going out to play with anyone than in daydreaming at home alone. She much preferred spending time in her own fantasy world, and would love nothing better than to dress her beloved tabby cat Mickey in one of her homemade tutus, if he would stay still long enough. He had quickly cottoned on to this ritual humiliation and tried to make a dash for the bottom of the garden whenever he saw the beaming girl approaching, armed with a costume. She practiced her best dance moves with her poor, bemused cat, to a musical accompaniment, and usually during a prolonged bout of joyful giggling.

Mickey generally slept in Kate's room, either curled up at the end of the bed or nuzzling against her under the covers, and he featured in most of her favourite dreams: Sometimes the two of them would be running a Dance Academy, giving demonstrations of their routines. At other times they would be involved in a Hollywood musical, dancing alongside the girl's favourite stars. However, her favourite scenario involved them dancing together on stage during a sold-out tour, she in an elegant dress and her cat looking dapper in top hat and tails. The pair always received rapturous applause from an enthralled audience which comprised adults, children and a variety of small animals and cartoon characters.

The girl begged her parents to let her have ballet lessons, offering to forgo all her pocket money for the duration of her childhood. She also asked for dancing shoes for several birthdays. Kate quickly progressed to taking part in local competitions, which she often won. Family and friends would come to watch her, and she relished performing in front of any kind of audience, playing to the gallery on every occasion. Her motivation was so strong and the adrenaline rush so exhilarating. She drove herself to practice for several hours every day, reading all the dancing books she could find and doing anything she could to improve her skills and increase her experience, ignoring the aches and pains that came along with her success.

Kate was an only child, and her wealthy lawyer parents were keen to help and support her towards achieving her dreams, but they also wanted to ensure that she appreciated the value of money and did not become spoilt. However, they were delighted to see that she was growing up to be a delightful, sensible, caring and considerate young woman. When she enrolled on a course in Performing Arts at the local College, they decided to splash out on a second-hand car to give her a taste of independence. The teenager was, of course, elated about this incredibly generous gift. Not only did she use her car every day, but she was also happy to give lifts to her friends.

She loved the course, especially the practical elements. During the first year, Kate developed a keen interest in ballroom dancing. She embraced its timeless elegance and grace, and worked very hard to master the techniques to perfection, living for losing herself in each movement and vibrant moment on the dance floor. It was at a special evening of ballroom dancing that one of the young men asked her out on a date. The young woman had danced with him many times, liked him very much, and felt a thrill of embarrassed excitement at having been asked. However, she had mixed feelings and had told him she would think about it and let him know the next day.

As she drove home that evening, Kate was barely aware of the high winds and heavy rain buffeting the car because her mind was spinning with fevered excitement and anticipation. She knew she was becoming very accomplished at ballroom dancing, and wondered if it would be possible to master other styles and ultimately be able to pursue a career in an activity that she loved so much. She had just started to question herself about whether she wanted to risk diluting the pure joy of dancing with the distraction of a relationship, and possibly jeopardise a pleasant friendship, when a cat suddenly appeared from nowhere out of the darkness into her headlights just as she was approaching a very sharp bend.

The woman had been driving down the familiar country lane a bit too quickly in the rapidly deteriorating weather conditions, and had no time to think. Her desperate attempt at an emergency stop led to the car skidding off the wet road and into a sickening head-on collision with a tree. Kate was killed instantly. A Persian cat, totally unscathed, stood looking at the mangled wreckage for a few moments, watching the wisps of smoke disperse and the back wheels until they stopped turning. She rippled her fur against the raindrops which were falling on her body, and then ambled back into the wood from which she had just emerged.

(ii) Cat Lady (1935 - 2015)

Richard Seal in Story Telling

The elderly lady had always been more than happy living alone. During her long life, Katherine had made many friends and saw them from time to time, but only when it suited, and strictly on her terms. She tended to lose touch with people when they moved away, and reserved the right to cancel any arrangements at the last moment if she felt like it. While she was generally quite friendly, and could be loving when she chose to be, the woman had a tendency to turn cool towards people on a whim. She was content about having a reputation for being somewhat enigmatic, sometimes aloof, and always fiercely independent.

Katherine had shared the majority of her life with a series of cats. Every one of them had been so precious, such unique and unforgettable characters. She felt that she had never fully recovered from the trauma of losing her first cat, a grey tabby called Emma, to an evil hit-and-run motorist when she was only five. It had taken nearly two years before she could even consider having another fur baby in her life. Jezebel, a tortoiseshell beauty with a permanently damp nose and tiny ears, had seen her through her teenage years, listening without judgement even during her final illness. How could she ever forget mottled Mr Mistopheles, whose timeless wisdom had been reflected in his every gesture and expression for over twenty years? Every one of them was irreplaceable, and without exception she preferred them to people.

The only annual social event that Katherine made a point of attending was a Halloween party held by her neighbour. Never caring what clothes other people might be wearing, she would don a different cat costume on each occasion. The woman would spend many months creating her outfit, lingering lovingly over the sewing and finer points of embroidery, taking her time to ensure the design and colour of each paw was just right. The tail needed to be crafted properly, each whisker straightened and configured, while the shape and size of such key features as her nose and ears could not be overlooked. Every year she would slink around the room in her cat guise for a while, selecting a few items from the buffet to put into the special bowl that she always brought with her; she did not mingle as such or speak to other guests, preferring to retreat to watch proceedings from the safe distance of the comfiest looking sofa. She would never announce her departure, slipping away silently as soon as she started to feel bored or could think of a better place to be.

Richard Seal in Story Telling

On her final night Katherine dozed off a couple of times while watching TV, feeling more weary than usual. She managed to muster enough strength to take herself to bed early, but she slept lightly and awoke with a start around midnight. Looking around the room, the lady could not see anything out of the ordinary, but sensed that something was amiss and she now felt wide awake and fully alert. She fancied having a snack before trying to go back to sleep, so decided to go downstairs to get something for herself and also see if her feline friends might be interested in some water and a few biscuits themselves.

Upon entering the living room, the woman stopped for a moment to inspect the room. She wrinkled her nose, rubbed her eyes gently then opened them wide in the darkness. Katherine had become accustomed to being able to see quite clearly at night without needing to turn on the light or even put on her glasses. The striking black and white light and shadows reminded her of an atmospheric film noir from the 1940s. While there were no famous Hollywood actors in this particular scene, her cats were always the main characters, her protagonists. They were all looking at the lady, blinking softly and kneading various items of the furniture in rapt anticipation.

Richard Seal in Story Telling

The woman started padding towards the kitchen, but after just a few steps she was suddenly struck by debilitating shooting pains. She pulled up, rooted to the spot in shock, gasping, then helplessly clutching her chest, before slumping heavily back onto the settee. Breathing fitfully now and finding her nightdress had quickly become drenched in a profuse sweat which was running alternately fiery hot then as cold as stone, Katherine could feel her consciousness starting to slip away, her senses fading. Her faltering hands reached out to touch and stroke the beloved cats, giving her the familiar warmth of joy, inner peace and relief.

Veteran campaigner Ginger's drilling slowly started up, like a well-oiled motor running smoothly on a sub-zero winter's morning, an engine so efficient and never likely to stall. As ever, his little sister Lily languidly cleaned her pristine white fur and would stretch all her limbs and twitch her tail several times before deigning to purr. Little black kitten Thomas flexed his tiny claws, then dribbled happily, accepting the lady's affection while lying on his back; then a moment later he was beady-eyed, pupils dilating, standing bolt upright, on sentry duty; in another instant he was gone, heading for the shadows behind the curtains, without looking back.

The next day, a neighbour, who was concerned that Katherine had given her apologies for the previous night's Halloween party, decided to check on her and bring her a piece of cake. As she entered the house she was shocked to find that the poor old woman had passed away. The neighbour had known the lady for a long time, but she had never felt very close to her, and she had no idea about who the next of kin might be. She was familiar with the three cats in the living room, they looked content and very well as ever. They were lounging around on the armchairs, focused on the task of grooming themselves thoroughly.

However, the neighbour was surprised to see a fourth cat in the room, a sleek Persian with striking, sharp blue eyes. She was standing a short distance away from the others, next to the television, which was showing an old film featuring Fred Astaire and Ginger Rogers dancing cheek-to-cheek. The cat looked away from the black-and-white images just for a moment, to give the intruder a marked look of indifference, before returning her gaze to the screen.

Captured

Overawed at sunset, annoyed
that the bleeding red streaks
of cloud, offset by softer pinks,
the violent oranges slashing at
the twilight sky, every feature
a one-off, is not quite the same
on film - To man seems absurd
nature refuses to be captured
via image or the written word.

....

As mist descends walls
brace themselves, mountain darkens.
House is swallowed whole.

....

Snail emerging from
his shell, is oblivious
to the hiker's boot.

Taking Hold

It was one of those July afternoons when the light seemed to be extra bright, emanating from somewhere else somehow, and the colours of everything around her appeared more vivid. On such a lazy hazy day, Alice could not help but wonder why it was necessary to be at school. The lower sixth form internal exams were over, and everyone knew that the next year was the really significant one. The dying days of this summer term just felt like marking time.

At lunchtime she decided to give her classmates the slip and spend some time doing some reading and possibly write a little poetry. Alice was half way through 'The Great Gatsby', and was totally enraptured by it. She had not told her friends about her writing, doubting that they would be very interested. In fact, she did not particularly like any of the girls, and could not care less about parties, clothes and shoes. Moreover, her feelings about love and relationships were too personal to be shared with them.

Alice wandered down to the far corner of the playing fields, beyond the reach of football games and any chattering huddles, and found a cool spot in the shade of a huge oak tree. She put 'Gatsby' in her lap for a moment and gazed out over the fields beyond the low fence: were they looking back at her, just as they had done to countless wistful teenagers over the centuries? The girl luxuriated in the thought, aware that an idea was taking hold in her consciousness.

She removed a single sheet of folded blank paper from between the leaves of her book. The girl breathed deeply in anticipation of losing herself in another world, feeling the magic as the poem runs away with itself, and is no longer in her control. By the end of that hour Alice had resolved to always find time for things which enrich existence and nourish the spirit. She felt sure Gatsby would approve.

Standing

So relieved to see oak tree
he kicked balls against, hid
behind, sat reading beneath
in his own shade pool is still
holding its own on the green.
The great roots remind him
of coiled serpents on guard,
poised to strike, bite, inject
a dose of poison into a fool
who might try to take it away
after two centuries standing.

.. ..

Cat's Servant

Cat rubs her face always
on Servant's leg - loves her
until the lunch arrives, then
reserves judgement whilst
lying grooming in the sun.
When called at dusk, sniffs
and strolls a pace beyond
woman's grasp. Often dines
elsewhere, has sleepovers,
disappears at will. Owning
her human, Puss will stay
while it is going her way.

*Too long spent fretting
about roots, until today:
time to embrace grey.*

Hoarder

Jenny moved the pile of magazines on the settee over a little to accommodate her ashtray. She stood up slowly and shuffled through the living room, edging slowly around the stacked cardboard boxes and stepping over the plates and cups on the floor. Before the woman had the chance to squeeze her way through the door, she heard the doorbell ring. For a moment she toyed with the idea of ignoring it, but a familiar voice put paid to that.

"Hello mum it's Maggie, let me in!"

Jenny trudged to the door, and opened it to find her middle aged daughter looking as harrassed as ever.

"Hello, dear."

Maggie kissed her mother briefly, but quickly turned her attention to the state of the house. "I know I haven't been here for a while, but this place looks worse than ever! There is rubbish everywhere, no room to move. How can you stand it? What do you need these things for?" She picked up one of several carrier bags lined up in the hall.

"This is my house, and these are my things. Please put the bag down." Jenny's voice quavered, and her hand shook slightly as she reached out to Maggie.

"Fine, I might catch something!" She dropped the bag. She took a deep breath and tried to calm herself down. "Look mum, this isn't normal. I don't think you're well."

"Stop patronising me, I know what I'm doing. If you want to call me a hoarder, go ahead. I'm not doing anyone any harm."

"Yes, But .."

"Have you come to see me or to give a lecture? I don't tell you how to live your life, do I?"

The two women settled on a tense truce and managed to find a little space to have a cup of tea at the kitchen table. The conversation was perfunctory, until Maggie got up to leave. Frowning hard, she put her hand on the old woman's arm.

"I'm sorry that I got angry, mum, it's just that I care and worry about you. Especially since dad died."

The lady nodded and patted her hand gently "I know you do, love, but I'm fine. I appreciate that the house isn't very tidy, but I am quite happy here."

After her daughter had gone, Jenny left the used cups on

the table, and draped a tea cloth over them. She lit a cigarette as her mind settled on Derek. Thoughts had never strayed too far from her husband in the five years since he had passed away. A smile spread across her face, accompanied by a few tears as she negotiated her way back into the living room to search for a TV programme that they had enjoyed together. Only half the screen was visible due to the heap of newspapers nearby.

Jenny had been on the waiting list for an operation for several months. When the date was finally confirmed, Maggie tried to put the anxious lady's mind at rest by reassuring her that the house would be fine without her for a few days. She stressed she would leave things as they were, and just check the post a couple of times. However, she had decided to spring a nice surprise on her mother - With the help of two friends, she cleaned the place from top to bottom and filled two skips with the obvious junk, putting the other things into some kind of order and away into cupboards and drawers wherever possible.

Maggie had not expected such an underwhelming response to all her efforts. Her mother seemed to be struck dumb by the shock of arriving back to a neat and tidy house. After standing in complete silence for several minutes, Jenny had managed to mumble a few words of thanks, but said very little else as she slumped down onto the settee and stared into space. It was only after her daughter had made her excuses and left, that the old woman finally allowed herself to break down and cry uncontrollably.

Over the next few weeks, Maggie noticed that her mother was either not returning her calls or making excuses as to why it was not convenient for her to come round. However, eventually Jenny told her daughter that she wanted to get out of the house a bit more and suggested they meet at a cafe for coffee and a chat once a week. It turned out to be a great idea, as the two women seemed to get along better than they had done for years. The old lady was feeling so much more secure and at ease now that her precious things were all around her again, back in view in their rightful places.

Leaves, curled over brown,
swirl around apples, grounded
rotting into soil.

....

Spider working hard
on the web, glances at fly
bound up for her lunch.

Cranky

Old man was always called
'Cranky' by kids next door.
Took him ages to return ball
when kicked over his hedge.
Seemed to mumble grumble
at them under his breath ...
Why was he such a misery?
Will limped out into garden
battling arthritis alongside
recurrent gout, keen to help
children resume their game.
Tried a friendly hello in vain,
but they ran off, he coughed
left standing alone in pain.

....

Old Lady

The young man and woman seemed to have spent some time
dithering at the end of the elderly lady's drive. They were
dressed in business suits, and both wore stormy
expressions as they argued with each other in the late
September sunshine. The woman was remonstrating with
her partner, with considerable head shaking and hand-

wringing. The man stood still, and looked impassive, almost nonchalant. As Phyllis watched them carefully through a crack in the curtains, she could hear the kettle coming to the boil. She retired to the kitchen to fill the teapot and selected a flowery cosy before heading for the front door.

The couple were taken aback to see the door open just before they had actually reached it. Struggling to regain her composure, the woman fiddled with her hair for a moment, and then started to speak in a slightly faltering voice. "Good morning, madam, my name is Jill and this is my colleague, Alan.."

"Yes, I'm sure it is," Phyllis spoke quietly. "I've been expecting you. Well, you'd better come in, hadn't you?"

Alan looked at Jill doubtfully, then turned to the old woman. "Well, madam, let me just say .. "

"Come inside to make your speech, young man. I'm not prepared to have a conversation on my doorstep."

The couple walked in, exchanging another questioning glance with each other. Phyllis took their jackets, which they surrendered without comment, then she ushered them into the living room and directed them towards the settee.

"Take a seat, and make yourself comfortable. I'll be back in a moment with the tea."

As she walked back into the room with a tray laden with tea and biscuits, Phyllis could see that they had been having a snatched conversation in her absence. They looked edgy, the young man appeared flustered and the woman's eyes darted from side to side a couple of times. The atmosphere was tense.

"Come on now, relax. You've made it into the house now haven't you? I don't suppose you get this far too often." She poured the tea, and selected an armchair opposite them, close to the door. "Do either of you take sugar?"

The young woman spoke quickly. "We would like to offer you a wonderful opportunity ... "

"Oh yes? What would you like to sell me, dear? A free holiday, perhaps?" She handed the woman a cup of tea. "I have the feeling that you haven't got any encyclopaedias with you. Do help yourself to biscuits."

Having sipped her tea, Jill looked anxiously at the lady. "We're not selling anything .."

Phyllis cut her off gently "Yes, I do appreciate that you're not actually sales people. I daresay that you're not using your real names either, but it doesn't matter." She paused before continuing. " I fear that I have put you both off your stride somewhat. I have disrupted your rehearsed routine, haven't I?"

"I don't know what you're going on about", Jill spoke now with clear irritation. "What kind of game are you playing?"

"Now, now, young lady. Your professional patter and politeness seems to be slipping already. I am not playing any games with you, after all I am just a defenceless old woman that the two of you have targeted to turn over. Tell me, whose job was it to distract me while the other slipped off to rifle through my meagre belongings?"

As they sat looking at her in stunned silence, Phyllis spoke again. "Now, dears, I don't want there to be any unpleasantness between us. In case you're thinking of trying to overpower the feeble pensioner, let me just introduce a little friend that I've brought along." She reached into her handbag and withdrew a small handgun. "There now."

The man spoke first, struggling to catch his breath. "Look, lady, we don't want any trouble .."

"I'm very pleased to hear that, Alan." She fixed her gaze on him, and patted the gun "My friend and I would like you both to stay and chat for a while. Why don't you tell me a little about yourself."

Jill started to get to her feet. "I've had enough of this, come on ... "

"Sit down please, Jill, I'm asking you nicely. We'll talk in a few minutes, I want to speak to Alan first." She sat down and glared at Phyllis.

"Well, I don't really know what I'm supposed to say," the man spoke quietly.

"Don't be shy, young man, could you tell me a little about your studies or your career, if you don't mind."

"My career .. ?" He looked sad suddenly. "I don't have a career." He looked down at his feet, before continuing wistfully "I have always wanted to be an actor really, I loved performing as a kid."

"That sounds like fun .."

"I loved it! I did shows for my parents, writing lines for my little sister too. I was in the school play, playing the female lead (it was an all boys school), then later on I joined an amateur dramatics group for a while. It was a wonderful experience." His voice got quicker and quicker as his excitement increased.

"Did you carry on with the acting, Alan?"

"No .. My parents were never keen on it. They eventually persuaded me to study to be an accountant, get myself a steady career." His voice had now dropped into a dull, flat tone.

"Did you enjoy accountancy?"

"I really didn't enjoy it at all. It was a very difficult course, exhausting, tedious and boring. I ended up dropping out after just a few months .. "

"How did that make you feel?" Phyllis spoke soothingly as she poured him another cup of tea.

"Terrible! I felt so depressed. Everything started to look so negative, black, and I just couldn't pull myself out of a deep hole for a long time."

"And what does life look to you now?"

"Well, I met Jill a few months ago, and she's helped me to get back on my feet." He grinned suddenly, turning to the young woman, who looked nonplussed.

"That's nice, Alan. I am so pleased for you." Phyllis caught his partner's eye. "Jill has obviously made you happy and she must be such a good influence on you. Will you start acting again?"

"I don't know, it could be .."

The young woman interjected, her eyes flashing. "I'm not stopping him, he can do whatever he wants! I know what you're trying to do, and it won't work on me. I'm not opening my heart to you, I don't care if you've got a gun!" She looked as if she was thinking of getting to her feet again.

"Keep calm, Jill, I really wouldn't want anyone to get hurt. Now, what do you want to talk about?"

"I don't want to talk to you about anything! Do you fancy yourself as some kind of gun-toting shrink?" She seethed at the old woman.

"Take your time, there's no rush. I'm happy to wait until you're ready. Perhaps you could tell me a little about your family."

"Okay, you win! My parents are divorced and I've got one sister. So what? Are you happy now? Go ahead, analyse that!"

"Do you get on well with them?"

"Not that it's really any of your business, but my dad died when I was a child if you must know, and mum got remarried. I haven't seen her for years."

"I'm sorry .. "

"I'm not! She chose to marry a violent, controlling pig and then neglected her own kids. She doesn't care about us. The woman can rot in hell as far as I'm concerned."

"Have you told your mum how you feel about the situation? You could call her if you'd prefer not to meet."

"No way! She knows where I am if she can spare the time to get in touch."

Richard Seal in Story Telling

"How is your sister?"

"She's fine, she's always fine! She's the best in fact - she had always been number one in everyone's eyes, and she makes sure that you know it ... Helen has never been interested in me and my life. She's the oldest, the prettiest, the clever one, the head teacher, the one with a lawyer husband and perfect kids, and I am just ..." Her voice was starting to crack.

"What are you, Jill?"

"I'm nothing." She put her head in her hands for a few moments, then looked up with tears in her eyes. "I am nothing and I'm going nowhere."

"What would you like to do, if you are given the chance?"

"When I was growing up I always wanted to be a nurse, look after people, but there's no chance of doing that now is there?"

"Don't you think so, you're still young .. "

"Yes, but I was hopeless at school, I failed all my exams. It could never happen for me .. "

Richard Seal in Story Telling

Phyllis settled back into her chair. "Right, I'm going to tell you both a little story about myself now. I have always loved writing, mainly poetry and short stories, about my life, my thoughts and feelings about family, friendship, nature, animals. My parents told me that it was a complete waste of time, my late husband thought the same way though he never actually said so. For decades I wrote in longhand in countless notebooks, or tapped away in my bedroom on my ancient typewriter. I entered numerous competitions, sent letters to publishers and agents, submitted material to endless magazines. Guess how many pieces I've had published over all these years."

They looked at her blankly, Jill shook her head slightly. "None. Not a single one. I've had absolutely no success on that front, receiving standard rejection slips left, right and centre. However, I've never stopped writing because I do it for myself. I enjoy it, writing consumes me, it completes my life. It's who I am. You need to ask yourselves who you are, and think about what you want from life."

"Why don't you do some research, explore your options. Talk to each other calmly and rationally about following a different way forward together. Acting, nursing are possible routes aren't they? Why not?" She looked at them both as they sat quietly, lost in thought. "We all do what we really want to do in life you know, and we can always find time for the things that genuinely mean something special to us. If you don't try to achieve your goal, you don't really want it badly enough. Today is the day to start following your dreams. Anything less is just an excuse."

Phyllis stood up, and led the couple out into the hallway. Neither were speaking now, and both looked contrite and introspective as the old woman helped them on with their jackets and walked with them to the front door. "Off you go, try to do something productive with your lives, be creative, positive - anything which makes you feel happy, fulfilled, better about yourselves and each other. It's never too late."

She watched them walking down the drive, and noticed that they were holding hands as they went through the gate. The woman closed the door, put the latch on, and smiled as she caught sight of the sideboard upon which she had placed the wallet, purse, and two mobile phones which she had removed from the jacket pockets. She pointed the gun towards her face, then pulled the trigger of the novelty lighter and lit one of Jill's cigarettes. She inhaled deeply before returning to the living room to switch on the TV and see if there was any more tea left in the pot.

Scrap paper scattered, crooked houses, twisted trees crayon-created.

....

Sticks

Steve was so glad that he had taken early retirement, and had moved with his wife away from London to the tranquility of the Spanish countryside. It was taking him some time to get used to no longer working for up to fifty hours a week as a harassed foreman in charge of a large team of men. Tina missed her grown up children a little more than she wanted to tell her husband, but she loved nature, the idyllic mountain setting, and relaxed way of life. Both of them felt calmer and more at peace.

Since their arrival, Steve had been intrigued by the tumbledown finca nearby. The building always looked dark, the shutters pulled down, and he had never seen any signs of life. He had wondered if it might be abandoned, but the front door looked solid and smoke occasionally appeared from the chimney. Each time the idea surfaced to go over there with

Richard Seal in Story Telling

Tina to introduce themselves, something always stopped him dead in his tracks. An unsettling feeling lurked in the pit of his stomach.

During a chilly spell in November, Steve finally decided that he had put off the inevitable long enough and it was high time that the central heating was fired up. As he paced up and down the gravelled drive one blustery afternoon, whilst waiting for an oil delivery, the man was suddenly aware of some movement over at the finca. He saw the front door open very slowly and a tiny figure stood in the doorway for what seemed like several minutes before starting to shuffle through the steadily lengthening shadows.

The old lady was wrapped in layers of black clothing. She blended in with the   darkening landscape to such a degree that she took on the appearance of a scurrying creature whilst bending deep over the undergrowth and filling her bag. When the huge truck arrived and sounded its horn, the woman barely seemed to flicker; she just pulled her scarf a little tighter against the wind and continued collecting sticks. When the delivery truck left, the woman was gone. Steve hoped she had enough wood to build a good fire. He knew that he would now feel reassured at the sight of the smoke.

....

Dyed

She has been blond for decades,

but turning fifty, Jill frowns back

at her own reflection, now vexed

about what hair colour to try next.

Her hair was brownish as a child;

lacking a style, she let it go wild;

Loved messing about, glad to let

mother's plaits and pigtails fall out.

In her teens tried dye with friends,

obsessed with lads and split ends;

After too long fretting about roots,

she will try another way: liberation

here to stay, time to embrace grey

....

Penny

His heart lurches when he hears her voice. Tony stands to meet his childhood crush who is travelling by train for the first time with her six year old daughter and four year old son. Sitting together again, twenty five years on, he nuzzles into lavender scent tingles. Seeing that familiar coy smile, he wonders if Abigail could forget her children for a short while, run across the fields and climb that stile with him again ..

.. Tony quickly reverts to falling down with her onto the cut grass, school field clumps hurled at each other. Her Alice band stolen briefly, he held it aloft with unbridled glee, her arms and long dark hair flailing in laughter. Abigail gave him a penny, slightly sticky, sealing the deal with a little liquorice kiss. It was only the fear of being too girly that held him back from sharing his six pence Curly Wurly.

The last time they had met had been a couple of years later in the park, just before her family had moved away. The chain's swing felt cold on his fingers. Laughing, pushing her too hard, Abigail almost came off with a shriek and promises of sweet revenge. Swapping places, Tony had relished her hilarity as the plastic seat had snapped beneath him.

As her stop approaches, the soft lines of laughter melt back into wedding rings, dark glasses are put on again, and hands touch farewell. He still has her coin though, saved in a match box.

AUNT

George was beginning to wish that he had let his parents contact a house removal company rather than offering to do it himself. The process was taking its toll on his patience and energy levels, and he was finding it almost impossible to move the dressing table on his own. However, the man was stopped in his tracks at the sight of an old fading photograph of his Aunt Jane. This forgotten picture in its faded frame with a crack in the glass must have slipped behind the heavy piece of furniture a long time ago.

The woman's smiling image still seemed to emanate her distinctive jasmine scent. Jane seldom spoke or seemed to understand any of her brother's jokes, she tended to smile to herself slightly, before turning away shyly to contemplate her cup of tea. However, she always had a kind word and a sweet or two for her nephew and niece. A navy blue handkerchief stored up her sleeve never seemed to be used, but was always there. George sometimes used to wonder if she kept a supply of them in her handbag.

During a visit that final summer, Jane had suddenly picked up one of the toy cars that her nephew was playing with, and put it in her pocket. As George had looked up in shock, the woman took the boy aside, and addressed him in hushed, conspiratorial tones. She had explained the importance of staying close to his family, and cherishing good thoughts and feelings about them whatever happened. Checking that they were alone, his Aunt had grasped the boy's hand with a sense of urgency before continuing, almost in a whisper:

"You might not be able to see your loved ones all the time, but it doesn't mean that they aren't there or don't care. They will always be with you, you just need to know how to look - be aware, my dear George, they will be there."

He had looked blankly at her for a moment, not sure what to say. This seemed to spur her on:

"You may not really understand what I'm saying to you at the moment, George, but these words will come back to you in the future and you will know."

"But, Aunt Jane, I'm not..."

She started speaking more quickly. "As you get older, think

about what you want to do and where you want to go, then do it. Don't wait for the world to make you an offer, make things happen. Embrace your dreams, don't let them fade away or settle for a life of mediocrity."

At that point, the boy's sister had entered the room, and Jane had reverted in an instant to her customary mild-mannered platitudes.

"Wash your hands now, George, we will be having tea in a few minutes."

Before he left the room, though, the boy noticed that there was a glint in her pale blue eyes for a fleeting second. That memory returned to him vividly now.

As the boy grew up, Aunt Jane's words stayed with him and remained an inspiration. George had not always had the easiest relationship with his parents, and his sister had some dogmatic opinions which grated on him at times. However, the young man had resolved to adopt a positive approach, and remained tolerant, calm and conciliatory with his family. He also took the decision to abandon his accountancy degree, which he hated, to devote his life to his passion for music. George loved teaching the subject at

high school, and writing and performing his own songs.

Thirty years had now passed since that April day when the lady vanished, after leaving her cottage for her morning walk in the Sussex countryside. There had been unconfirmed sightings of her in different towns over the first few months, and fanciful rumours about the lady's whereabouts circulated amongst the family for a number of years. George placed the frame back onto the dressing table for a moment, and looked at it again. His aunt looked so happy sitting in her favourite chair in the living room, stroking her beloved white cat ...

... Two months later George managed to persuade his wife that an idyllic place to stay during their annual summer holiday would be Collioure, a small town on the Mediterranean coast of Southern France. Initially unconvinced about the idea, Elaine became particularly interested when he told her that his research had revealed that it had been a popular retreat for Paris' artists at the start of the twentieth century, and the location appears in the paintings of Henri Matisse. They agreed to go in

August during the annual Saint Vincent festival.

Fortunately, the place turned out to be even more beautiful than George had hoped. The couple had been able to relax together in the charming bars and cafes, they enjoyed the stunning coastal views from the medieval Château Royal de Collioure, and also took in the seventeenth century Notre-Dame-des-Anges Church. On the afternoon before the festival started, Elaine decided to spend a couple of hours exploring the Modern Art Museum, while her husband visited a local cat sanctuary.

When the forty-year-old man and the elderly owner, a delightful woman with a twinkle in her eyes, saw each other they were both stopped in their tracks for almost a minute before falling into a long embrace. Close to tears, George found that he had so much to say to the lady, who was overjoyed to see him. They had a wonderful time sharing stories and laughter over home made cakes and a pot of tea. On the mantelpiece there were several family photographs, alongside a very old, red toy racing car...

. . . .

Hugged

**During hugs Joyce always holds
on too tight, seems to squeeze
with all her might, demonstrating
infectious happiness, her feelings
ever joyous, warm, unrestrained.
Although elderly now, Joyce is full
of that same passion and a zest
for life that she has always had:
desire to kiss cheeks, seize hands
and hope everyone understands.
It seems unlikely she will refrain
from sharing all her love, casting
aside stick or Zimmer frame.**

··············

In final moments,
sees daisy chains, snowman made
wearing best mittens.

··············

Woman drifting sees
moth bouncing off bulb, flickers
once, then goes out.

Moon

**As a girl, loved staring
up at the moon, knowing
she would travel there
one day, not too soon.
So mysterious, inviting
it always looked exciting.
Each night now old lady,
despite her failing sight,
goes back with utter joy
to the comfort of its light.**

....

Grave

Wandering through the graveyard, long since full, the woman never sees anyone else. The lank grass is too long, the moss has spent centuries infiltrating headstones, aiming to obscure and consign the deceased to oblivion evermore. She reads aloud a few names which are carved in stone - perhaps to be heard this final time before they spend an eternity alone.

Tracing her fingers around one particular green and grey-tinged name brings the man back to life more than a century on. Joseph Hill had been a miner, man and boy, just like his old dad, battling to give his family some of the things that he had never had; struggling to

---

stay alive, destined never to thrive, expiring after a long shift, dust-covered at fifty five ...

The small bunch of flowers which look like they have been placed at the graveside recently. Perhaps this was a man, beloved by his family and friends, whose legend has continued to live on through the successive generations and many joyful relations ... She senses deep warmth, thinking about Joseph and his workmates laughing in the pub, playing a game of darts, and downing pints of bitter after work.

....

Market Day

Mum loved Market Day .. She would wrap her little lad and then herself up in long scarves, thick gloves, and voluminous duffel coats to brave the sub-zero temperatures and harsh winds which could often be found whistling around the stalls. The blast seemed to take the greatest delight in finding the slightest gap in their layers of winter clothing. Only the regular traders had seemed unmoved by the unforgiving conditions, hardened as they were to a hustle-bustle life of all-weather ducking and diving.

The pair would joyfully face the surround-sound barrage of banter; the quick-fire patter left the boy feeling amused and confused: Alongside hearing about the finest Granny Smith

apples in the land, and purchasing plum tomatoes so ripe and grand, they were subjected to offers on oranges you would be a fool to refuse. Mum was usually tempted to bring home more cheap carrots than she could ever use. After choosing some good value mince to last the whole week, she gave a bag to her little man to carry. This added even more roses to his chubby cheeks.

Forty years on Mark still goes to the same market, but everything has changed, been re-arranged, and it all feels rather strange. The place seems smaller, cleaner, quieter, more orderly and corporate somehow, and every stall is different now. However, a few of the products are intriguing: sometimes exotic, hailing from distant lands, with packaging with writing impossible to understand. Most of the past has gone, and yet the ghost voices of old traders echo on. The middle aged man knows his mum would have taken some of those lychees before they had all gone.

....

Music Box

On Granny's sideboard, nestling
between photographs ancient
and modern, below mysterious
Roman numerals clock, lost in
its own time, sat a box, almost
sepia, its music seldom played.
When she died, box departed,
tune never again to be started -
It went to niece, where is it now?
Probably no longer on display,
perhaps used as retro ash tray.

White

Final moments, face
whiter than her hair ...
Mind drifts through
clouds back to daisy
chains with friends;
cotton sheets, tucked
in by mum; cafe sugar
lumps, full fat milk;
last snowman made
wearing best mittens ...

Hat

Since childhood old chap
had always sported a hat -
His school cap exchanged
for teenage fedora, bobble
on chilly days, a ten gallon
during his cowboy phase,
a straw hat when strolling
through the fields; Finally
in senior years reverted
to cap. It was still in place
during his final nap.

Walking Woman

Polly had often wondered how much time she had spent over the
years sitting in either her bedroom or the front room of the
family home staring out of a window at the busy world passing
by. It had always been a strangely satisfying and comforting
pastime, a chance to disconnect from her own life just for a little
while and escape into the imagined life of other people. She had
always enjoyed inventing scenarios for a range of different
characters, which seemed to be even more fun if they looked
unusual, eccentric or a bit like a celebrity. However, there was
one particular woman who had always fascinated and intrigued
her. She had watched her walking up and down the road in front
of the house, on and off, for decades.

Richard Seal in Story Telling

As a child she would watch the harried-looking young mother scurrying along in an agitated fashion, appearing somewhat dishevelled. The lady would be trying to push an unwieldy-looking double pram while keeping an eye on two older children, who seemed to be lagging behind or running on ahead, and spend most of their time either in floods of tears or fighting each other. As this motley crew passed in front of Polly's window there would be a brief cacophony of conflicting sounds and a general hubbub before the street could return to some semblance of order.

During many long hours of self-imposed bedroom exile in her sometimes troubled teenage years, Polly would feel a degree of reassurance when looking down at the walking woman barely breaking stride on her daily route march to the school. She would shake her head anxiously whilst checking her watch and sometimes snatch a couple of drags on a cigarette. The lady's fraught return journey, now with several screaming or moaning children in tow, reminded the girl that things in her life were perhaps not so bad after all and before too long her latest of her dark moods would pass.

Visiting her parents a few years later, Polly, now a young mother herself, would still sometimes take time out to look through the window and smile when seeing the familiar figure of the walking woman still making her way down the road: Middle-aged now, and looking smarter and a lot less stressed than in her youth, the woman appeared to be enjoying a leisurely stroll and chat with a couple of her friends. Polly wondered if they might be en route to one of their favourite cafes in the town for tea and cakes, or perhaps they were heading to a pub to enjoy a couple of hours well-earned break from the tedium of life's routines.

A decade later, life seemed to be taking its toll on Polly as she approached her fortieth birthday. She was newly divorced, and often found it difficult to motivate herself or to enjoy her free time despite the fact that her children seemed to be increasingly preoccupied with their own lives. She enjoyed seeing her parents once a week during those difficult times, and noticed that the walking woman by now looked older, but kindly, assured and comfortable as she headed towards the post box clad in a thick winter coat which was perhaps a Christmas present from her children or she might have saved up and treated herself. Polly sometimes toyed with the idea of going out to say hello, or even ask her in for a cup of tea and a chat, but the moment always passed and instead she opted to make a move and drive home before the rush hour traffic got too bad.

Twenty further summers having passed in what seemed like no time at all, Polly found herself back at the family home and wrapped up in the thankless task of sorting through all the effects of her recently deceased parents, in the company of her two grown-up, and somewhat disinterested, children. Sitting near the front room window, she stopped in her tracks, dropping the stack of papers back into its cardboard box, at the sight of the walking woman. Her hair was now fashioned in a grey-white bun, pulled tight by pins; whilst she was stumbling, fumbling with her zimmer frame, as she edged painfully slowly along the same cracked pavement, she wore an expression of grim determination and resolve.

Suddenly the woman stopped and turned to look in Polly's direction for what felt like a long time. She looked unsteady on her feet, wavering slightly as the wind buffered her frail body. She looked so small and slight, and appeared almost translucent.

She imagined that the old woman might be a weightless, timeless mythical creature which exists in the shadowy region somewhere between a dream, a nightmare and a flight of fancy. The lady held her gaze then very slowly raised a hand. Polly froze for a moment as time stood still, then it felt like she was moving in slow motion as she returned the gesture. The walking woman lingered a little longer before looking away and resuming her faltering journey.

Less than two months later Polly was back on her home territory for what proved to be the final time, doing some final checks and removing the last of her mother's personal items from the house before the completion of the sale to a newly married couple of teachers. She sat in the front room with a last cup of tea from the large flowery teapot that her mum had only used on special occasions. The daughter looked out of the window with burning eyes as she clutched her mother's favourite blue nightie, lost in childhood memories. There was no sign of the walking woman that day, but after a few minutes she was surprised to see a balding middle-aged man approaching. He turned into the drive and nodded at her as he walked towards the front door. She frowned slightly as she opened it to the stranger.

"Hello, I'm so sorry to bother you..." The man shuffled his feet and smiled apologetically. He cleared his throat then paused and looked at her quizzically. "Are you Polly, by any chance?"

"Yes, I am. And you ..?" Suddenly she recognised a much older and greyer version of the scruffy little boy who had lived a few doors down the street during her childhood. He would chase her sometimes, making a grab for one of her long blond pigtails, but she had always managed to get away from him, leaving a trail of giggles behind her. "It's Frank, isn't it?"

He nodded, blushed slightly, and tentatively held out his hand for a moment, but then they opted for a slightly awkward hug instead. 'It's nice to see you again after all these years, Polly, I must say you still look the same."

"I wish." She rolled her eyes with a sheepish grin, fiddling with her hair. "You are very kind to say so though, Frank."

"I have some sad news, I'm afraid. Helen passed away the other day after a short illness." He shook his head, then broke eye contact with her for a few seconds before continuing. "I am calling on her old friends and neighbours and inviting them to the funeral at St James's Church - it was such an important place for her of course, she went there every Sunday throughout her life. The funeral service is next Friday - can you come? It would be so lovely if you could."

She hesitated. "I'm sorry. Helen .. ? Could you remind me who she was?"

"She was the elderly lady who lived at the end of this road for over fifty years. Everyone recognised her. Helen used to go everywhere on foot, you must have seen her walking to and fro along the street many times, often with her children. She told me several times that she always smiled to herself when she saw you watching her from the window."
The woman felt her stomach drop. She was still holding the nightie, which she now squeezed and instinctively lifted to press to her chest ...

A week later Polly found herself standing in a churchyard, bracing herself against the drizzle-laden breeze, feeling relieved that the funeral of the woman that she had never actually met and yet felt had always been in her life, was over. She could feel nagging twinges in her back and her flat feet ached from too much time spent standing and talking to people, both before and after the church service. It struck her that the aged vicar, who had stumbled over the deceased lady's name, did not appear to know very much about Helen.

After exchanging pleasantries with Frank and a few other familiar old faces from the neighbourhood, Polly had spent half an hour in the company of Helen's three adult children. They were all keen to stress that their mother had been such a loving, determined and independent woman, who had battled to hold down a series of part-time jobs cleaning and working in shops while trying to raise them alone. The lady had overcome her husband's untimely death in his thirties, then her youngest daughter had succumbed to leukaemia at the age of eight, but she had remained a tower of strength for her family. It was clear to Polly that these people were less focused on their grief than on sharing their positive and happy memories, and celebrating the life of a remarkable lady.

Feeling a little shaky, Polly was grateful to be able to lean against her son and take his arm for support. The woman was also glad to be distracted by her daughter chatting about her new job, as they walked together down the line of parked vehicles towards her car. Stopping to wince and wipe her glasses for a moment in the failing light that chilly October afternoon, she saw a pair of young eyes watching her from a house across the street. The little girl was only partly hidden by a twitching pink bedroom curtain, as she surveyed this ageing lady's laboured progress. Polly smiled thinly, looked towards the window and raised her hand. At that moment she realised that she was a walking woman too.

Amazed how a word
or line shifts into a shape,
then takes its own life.

Healing

Everything had seemed so different to Eric after Sally died. He was continuing to sit on the sofa watching the same television screen in the unchanged living room, where his wife's slippers were still beside her chair, but the frequency of life had changed, it had been subtly re-tuned to create a strange place with an alien face. They had had an enduring marriage, with unspoken love and intermittent laughter and joy.

Janet, Eric's daughter, has lived nearby for a couple of years, and she has been a great strength and support since Sally's final, protracted battle with the ravages of cancer. The middle-aged woman juggles her job in a shop with family life and keeping an eye on her father, bringing him an evening meal. Initially numb to everything, and unable to do anything more than go through the motions, acceptance was now starting to descend upon the bereaved man.

Richard Seal in Story Telling

Eric has never really wanted anything for himself, he had spent eight decades trying to provide for his wife and daughters, preferring to listen and react to other people's stories rather than creating his own. The man was now starting to stay in bed for longer and longer, finding some sanctuary hiding away beneath the sheets. The more concern his daughter expressed about his welfare, the more lethargic and listless he seemed to become.

The day that Marky arrived, Eric's pilot light showed signs of flickering back into life. An elderly neighbour had passed away leaving her twelve year old cat without a home, and Janet had volunteered her father into looking after him until something else could be arranged. Initially the old man felt anxious that he no longer had the ability or inclination to take care of himself, let alone an animal. His daughter reassured him that the cat would be good company, and not to worry.

The afternoon after his arrival, Marky padded up to the old man's bedroom. As he lay in limbo with his eyes closed, Eric could hear the light drilling sound and sensed it calming his nerves. He tentatively stretched out his hand, and it settled gently on the cat's back. Marky responded by deepening his purring and flexing his paws. As the vibration filled him with a relaxed energy, Eric drifted between sleep and a meditative state.

As each day starts with Marky's arrival and ends with him curled up at the end of the bed, existence seems more positive, and Eric spends more and more time living in the moment with his healing companion. Janet seems very happy to see them together too. The man feels free to appreciate just being, not speaking, and while he has no fears about the prospect of death, he now hopes that it does not arrive any time soon for him and his new friend.

Afloat

So long asleep, she woke to find
the whole World had gone blind -
No-one else could see how, why
this girl now seemed bright-eyed
and bushy tailed. She well knew
that all the medication had failed,
perhaps her own ship had sailed
yet in the darkness she had seen
something there, felt a presence
which kept her afloat, somehow
calmer and stiller, with one hand
retaining a firm grip on the tiller.

Living Now

Need to live supremely well
in the present, seize moments
to cherish as though our last.
Know too the past has gone;
Recall, at times, warm images
of joy, not pain to play again.
Need not dwell on future which
will never come - all we have
is the Now: Feel its power,
peace .. embrace being.

"Life can often be
like a Haiku - feelings, thoughts
hanging incomplete."

Percychatteybooks
Story Telling
Somerset House
6070 Birmingham Business Park
Birmingham
B37 7BF
Registered Number 2299335

www.percychatteybooks.com